Volume Nine

TOOLS

D1572782

Volume Nine

TOOLS

Curtis J. Badger

STACKPOLE BOOKS

Published by
STACKPOLE BOOKS
Cameron and Kelker Streets
P.O. Box 1831
Harrisburg, PA 17105

Printed in the United States of America

10 9 8 7 6 5 4 3 2 1

First edition

Interior layout by Marcia Lee Dobbs

*Cover design by Mark B. Olszewski
with Pam LaBarre*

Library of Congress Cataloging-in-Publication Data
(Revised for volume 9)

Badger, Curtis J.
    Bird Carving basics.

        Contents: v. 1. Eyes — v. 2. Feet — [etc.] — v. 9.
Tools.
        1. Wood-carving. 2. Birds in art. I. Title.
TT199.7.B33   1990   731'832   90-9491
ISBN 0-8117-2334-8 (v. 1)

Cover photographs by Curtis Badger

Contents

Acknowledgments

A project such as this series of books is indeed a team effort. I would like to thank everyone who has participated, especially the artists who have shared their time and talents with me.

Special thanks also go to Judith Schnell of Stackpole Books, who came up with the idea for the series and encouraged me to take on the project. Thanks also to Judith and other Stackpole editors and designers for turning my typed copy and photographs into a handsome, published product.

A special thanks with this volume on tools to Phil English and everyone at P. C. English, Inc., in Thornburg, Virginia. Phil opened his shop to me, helped set up tools for pictures, lent product shots, allowed me to monitor one of his carving seminars, and provided much good advice, especially for the chapters on wood and tools for decorative carving.

Thanks also to Grayson Chesser, Pete Peterson, Don Mason, Rich Smoker, Mark McNair, and all the other artists who have allowed me to aim my camera over their shoulders and who never complained when I asked for the dozenth time: "Just one more shot?"

Introduction

Some tools remove wood faster than others, some with more efficiency and safety. Some tools are designed to extract great masses of wood, and others are intended to remove just enough to create some subtle little detail, like a feather barb on a miniature carving of a songbird. But when you get right down to it, the purpose of all carving tools is the same: to remove all wood that doesn't look like a bird.

The tricky part is knowing what kind of bird you want to carve, how that bird should look, and which tools do the best job of achieving that look.

Old-time decoy makers used fairly unsophisticated woodworking tools, items often borrowed from cabinetmakers or other craftsmen. With only a sharp hatchet, drawknife, spokeshave, chisel, and a straight-edged knife they could turn out magnificent hunting decoys in a very short time.

Modern decoy makers do the same today. Indeed, part of the pleasure in making traditional hunting decoys is in using the traditional tools. There is a certain purity in using the old methods, a way of experiencing a part of American folk culture. The experience is probably not unlike playing bluegrass music on hand-made instruments. But if your goal in life is to carve a perfect replica of a chickadee on a holly branch, then a hatchet and drawknife are going to do you about as much good as a chain saw.

The moral of our story is that carvers must match the tool to the job, and the purpose of this book is to get you started in that direction. What follows is a discussion of carving tools—from traditional to state of the art—and an explanation of what they are intended to do and how carvers put them to use.

Your choice of carving tools will reflect the style of carving you do. This magnificent mallard drake was carved by Jett Brunet of Galliano, Louisiana. The exquisite feather detail was added with a variety of bits used with a flexible-shaft grinder. A burning tool—a sharp, heated blade—was used to etch each feather barb. Information on tools for decorative carving is included in chapter 4.

For making hunting-style decoys a few hand tools—a hatchet, drawknife, rasp, detailing knife—will suffice. Here, Pete Peterson rounds out a body with a drawknife, using a shaving horse to hold the workpiece. In chapter 3 you'll find more information on the shaving horse.

A bandsaw is handy for roughing out heads and bodies.

This book is designed to help you shorten the learning curve, to guide you in matching tool to task, and perhaps even to save you money by helping you to avoid purchasing tools you'll use once and eventually relegate to the attic. As you zero in on a particular style of carving, you'll also zero in on a fairly specific spectrum of tools. In other words, as you gain experience, you'll learn which tools work best for the type of carving you want to do.

Bird carving is a very individualistic art, and the tools that work well for one carver might not serve the needs of another. Just because champion carvers such as Larry Barth and Bob Guge use particular tools doesn't mean you should necessarily use the same.

When I was a little boy, I loved baseball, and Mickey Mantle was my hero. A local sporting-goods store had a baseball glove endorsed by Mickey Mantle, and I was certain that if I could earn enough money to buy that glove, I would be able to play center field like Mantle. So I mowed lawns, washed cars, and ran endless errands, and then, on one particularly glorious summer morning, I walked into that sporting-goods store, emptied my pockets, and marched out with the Mickey Mantle glove.

That afternoon we played a group of boys from another neighborhood, and in the third inning, with the score tied and runners on first and second, an opposing batter hit a long fly ball to me in center field. I raced back, looking over my shoulder to follow the arc of the ball, and just as I reached the fence, I raised my new Mickey Mantle glove, the ball hit squarely in the pocket, then dribbled out and landed on my foot. Two runs scored.

Traditional tools include this spokeshave, designed for shaping contours such as this head.

A drill press is used to hollow out working decoys.

Old-time decoy makers made do with the materials and equipment that were available. The late Doug Jester of Chincoteague, Virginia, paints a decoy on a wooden stump in his yard.

Brothers Lemuel and Steve (pictured here) Ward of Crisfield, Maryland, were considered two of America's finest carvers in the mid-1900s. The brothers worked in a fairly spartan shop, using hatchets, knives, rasps, and other conventional woodworking tools. Yet, they turned out beautiful and graceful bird carvings.

I learned that buying a particular glove was not going to make a Mickey Mantle of me, nor would I ever take over center field for the Yankees when Mantle's aching knees finally gave way.

In a similar way the art in bird carving does not come from tools but from a special vision, talent, knowledge of birds, and an awareness of spatial relationships. A good carving is a marriage of intangibles, such as vision and design, with very real objects, such as knives and wood.

In this book we'll deal with the knives and wood, hoping that you will learn to use them to produce your own individual statement on the beauty of birds, the drama of nature, and the poetry of flight.

1

Setting Up Shop

In working on the Bird Carving Basics series, I've visited dozens of carving shops and studios and have found that no two look alike. The tools may be similar, and even the birds produced may have similarities, but the workshops are as singular as the artists' personalities.

Indeed, a carver's workplace reflects his or her personality and style of carving. Some are scrupulously neat, with every tool in its proper place; others have the look of . . . well, ordered chaos might be a diplomatic description.

Shops usually reflect the style of carvings produced in them. Grayson Chesser makes hunting decoys, and his two-room workshop is filled with the wonderful aroma of cedar shavings and sawdust, which form a deep carpet in the vicinity of the bandsaw. Sunlight entering the room is nicely diffused by a layer of cedar dust on the windows, old decoys are piled on the floor, a deerskin hangs on the wall, a plumber's lead pot stands ready to make anchors and weights, and an old bathtub takes up one corner of the room. Grayson uses the tub to make sure his finished decoys float properly.

Grayson's shop is an eclectic mixture of tools, carving supplies, and various odds and ends. It's the shop of a decoy maker, not a carver of decorative birds. Take away the electric bandsaw and you could step back in time by a century or more. A heavy carving block is situated by the glass door for good lighting, and a hatchet, spokeshave, drawknife, and several chisels are nearby.

The room is filled with light, texture, and that wonderful aroma of cedar. It is a woodworking shop, a place where sensible, functional items are made by hand. And so it is with Grayson's decoys. They are made to be handled and used; their function is to lure ducks to the gun, not to sit on a mantel and look pretty.

To anyone other than Grayson, his workplace might seem to be a jumble of tools, wood blocks, glass eyes, paints, and debris from various past projects. But Grayson knows every dusty nook and cranny, and he turns out superb gunning decoys with great efficiency there.

Grayson Chesser in his carving shop.

A combination of form and function: Grayson's brant decoys as they were intended by the maker, floating on the open water. Your goals in bird carving will determine the tools you need. Do you want to make functional hunting decoys like these or decorative birds designed only for display?

Not all of Grayson's brants are intended to float, however. These stick-ups are functional hunting decoys, designed to be placed at the edge of the water.

Grayson's heron is a confidence decoy, intended to supplement a rig of working decoys at the water's edge as it's doing here, but it spends most of its time in a more decorative function: brightening the Chessers' flower garden.

3

The antithesis of Grayson's shop might be that of Jim Sprankle of Chester, Maryland, or perhaps Jo Craemer of Georgetown, Delaware. Jim is nationally known for his blue-ribbon decorative waterfowl, and his neat studio reflects his passion for order, detail, and preparation. His painting table overlooks an aviary, and on one wall are dozens of mounted birds to be used as reference material. A file cabinet contains detailed records of past projects. Jim keeps copious notes on each bird he paints, recording the mixtures of paint and the number of washes applied. His birds reflect his attention to detail and his dedication to excellence and precision.

Jo Craemer also is a carver of decorative birds, specializing in songbirds and raptors. Her workshop reflects the style of carving she does and also hints at her career before carving. Jo is a retired U.S. Navy nurse, and her work area is clean and well ordered, as if an inspection were scheduled at any moment. Tools are neatly arranged, the work area is well lighted, and files contain any reference material that might be needed.

The style of carving you choose to do—decoys, decoratives, interpretive sculpture—reflects your per-

Jim Sprankle's shop is clean, neat, and orderly, reflecting his style of carving, and includes separate rooms for carving and painting, ensuring that dust particles don't contaminate his painting area. An aviary is attached to his studio, as well as classroom space for holding carving workshops.

sonality and experience in life, and so does your workshop. A work area is a process of evolution; it cannot be created overnight. Sure, you can go out and spend a fortune on tools and supplies, but it's going to take a while to make your work space conform to your personality.

While a book such as this can't tell you exactly how to set up your shop, it can offer a few general guidelines that have to do with efficiency and safety.

Let There Be Light

All work areas should have good lighting. Every workshop I've ever visited—from spartan decoy-making shops to state-of-the-art studios—has shared this quality. Sometimes the light comes from large windows or glass doors, preferably facing north to avoid direct sunlight, but more frequently it is artificial.

Many carvers use two sources of light: an overall, broad source to provide general illumination for a room plus more concentrated light in a carving or painting area.

Fluorescent lights are popular because they offer broad, soft, but bright illumination, and they don't generate much heat. The problem with most fluorescents is that the color of light they produce is not close to that of daylight. This doesn't present much of a problem in a carving area, but it can be a difficulty at a painting station, where the mixing of colors is an exact science.

Fluorescents also do not lend themselves to color photography. Many carvers like to use a camera to document the progress of a bird, and fluorescent bulbs produce a sickly and unflattering greenish cast. The alternative is to use a supplemental light source, such as a flash, for the photos, or to use special fluorescent bulbs that approximate the color temperature of daylight.*

---

*Color temperature is a standard for defining the color of light based upon its similarity to the light color emitted by a black body heated to a known temperature. Color temperature is expressed in degrees Kelvin and applies to continuous-spectrum light such as that emitted by the sun, light bulbs, and so forth. A standard household tungsten bulb emits light of about 3,200 degrees Kelvin, while sunlight on a clear day is approximately twice that. Most photographic flash units produce light the color temperature of daylight.

So if you light your workshop with fluorescents, use bulbs that are balanced for daylight. Most electronic-supply stores or sellers of light fixtures stock them or will order them for you.

In addition to general illumination of your work area, you'll also want some concentrated light where you do complicated tasks such as detail carving and painting. Art-supply and office-supply stores have a wide range of lamps in various sizes and configurations. Many carvers prefer lights that clamp to a worktable or mount on a wall and can be adjusted to zero in on a particular work area.

Avoid high-wattage bulbs that emit a great deal of heat. Not only can they create an uncomfortable work area, they also can wreak havoc in painting by causing the paint to dry before washes of color can be blended.

Getting Rid of Dust

Eliminating dust from the workplace is important for several reasons. Foremost is one of health. Exposure to small dust particles can do serious damage to the respiratory system, and the paper dust masks sold in hardware stores are not sufficient to alleviate the problem.

Dust can also wreak havoc in your painting area when particles become embedded in thin washes of

Removing wood dust is important for health reasons and for maintaining a clean painting area. Don Mason built this system, which uses exhaust fans and filters to remove airborne particles. Note also the work light attached to the framework of the box.

acrylic paint. Suddenly, all that wonderful feather detail you worked so hard to replicate is obliterated.

Before buying that wonderful new electronic carving tool, invest in a good dust-removal system. Most of the carving-supply stores have them. The P. C. English Dust Box features two twelve-inch fans that suck dust-laden air through a system of filters at a rate of 650 cubic feet per minute. The Dust Box helps keep tiny wood particles out of your work area and, more importantly, out of your lungs.

Several companies make similar units, and some carvers have made their own, often using vacuum cleaners or fans to exhaust contaminated air from the workroom. Peruse the carving-supply catalogs (see Appendix) or attend carving shows to get a firsthand look at what is available. Select a dust-removal system that's comfortable and quiet to work with. Otherwise,

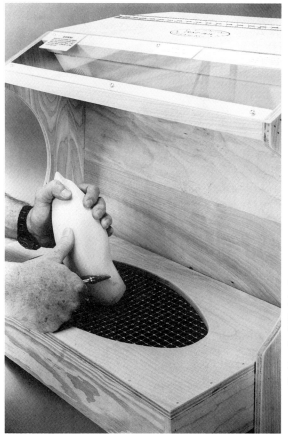

This is the P. C. English Dust Box, a dust-removal system designed and marketed by the Thornburg, Virginia, company. The Dust Box uses two twelve-inch fans and filters to remove small airborne wood particles.

you'll be tempted to go back to the dangerous method of inefficient masks or no protection at all.

Defining Your Space

Carving shops vary widely in size and layout. In most cases carvers use what happens to be available to them, be it a basement room, a spare bedroom, or a corner of the garage.

If possible, try to have separate areas for carving and for painting. Carving is a dusty, dirty job, and painting is just the opposite. In a carving area dust is pervasive, and you just can't get the area clean enough to do a good job of painting, especially if you intend to specialize in highly detailed decorative birds or miniatures.

A few dust particles in acrylic paint can do great harm to those carefully burned feather barbs you worked so hard to create. So try to separate the carving from the painting, even if it means painting in a spare corner of the bedroom or at the kitchen table.

A workshop should be fairly well organized. That is, when you need a certain bit for your Foredom tool, you should have a good idea where to find it. Methods of shop arrangement and tool storage are almost as singular as carving styles. Again, it is a process of evolution, of finding which method works best for you.

Carving-supply stores are good places to start. They offer various stands, shelves, clamps, vises, magnetic strips to hold metal tools and bits, and assorted other paraphernalia. Visit your local hardware store, hobby store, plumbing-supply store, even the housewares department of your local department store. And consult other carvers. Sharing ideas is an esteemed tradition in bird carving.

The amount of space you need will be determined by the kinds of carvings you do. If you plan to specialize in miniatures or in songbirds, then a fairly compact working area is called for. But if you want to do large pieces featuring several birds in elaborate settings, then you're going to need room to navigate. Keep in mind that the larger the area you have, the more difficult it will be to keep clean and the farther you'll have to walk to get that wood rasp you left on the other side of the room.

Your work space should reflect the style of carving you do. Grainger McKoy of South Carolina creates large, complex sculptural pieces and needs plenty of room in which to work. He designed and built his studio to fit his specific needs.

Pete Peterson of Virginia's Eastern Shore specializes in hunting-style decoys and shorebirds. His studio resembles an old-time carver's shop, right down to the shaving horse holding the decoy body he's working on here. For more information on the shaving horse, see chapter 3.

The Brunet shop in Galliano, Louisiana, is not only a workplace, it's also a family and community gathering spot. Five-time world champion Tan Brunet is seated at the worktable, flanked by sons Jude, left, and Jett, a two-time world champion.

I've seen workshops that vary from the size of closets to large studios. Grainger McKoy of South Carolina is an artist who specializes in large, complex works intended to be viewed from any angle. His studio is spacious and well lighted, with a high ceiling and ample space on all sides of his work-in-progress. He designed and built it himself, and it suits his needs perfectly.

Gary Yoder works in a small spare bedroom in his home in Grantsville, Maryland. Gary is a world-champion carver who specializes in miniatures and songbirds, so his ideal workplace is one that is compact enough to have all his tools close at hand.

The well-known Brunet family of Galliano, Louisiana, works in a converted boathouse. Tan Brunet moved the building to his home years ago when he took up carving full-time, and now he and his sons, Jett and Jude, work side by side. Often neighbors drop in to chat and work on carvings of their own, so their shop has a social function as well as a carving function. The room is dominated by a large table, and on most evenings four or five carvers will be gathered around, carving birds and talking about bird art.

About Safety

Bird carving is a relatively safe pursuit, but any field that places a premium on sharp edges and electronic gizmos should be approached with a modicum of common sense.

First, before rushing to the shop to try out that new EZ Carve Duck Buster, sit down, take a deep breath, and read the manufacturer's instructions. And don't skim over the safety section.

Always work with sharp cutting tools. Take the time to put an edge on that knife. If you aren't sure how to do it, we'll show you in chapter 3.

As mentioned earlier, protect yourself from airborne dust particles. This is especially important if you carve decorative birds and create a lot of fine detail, because this means you're also creating a lot of fine dust. Buy a good dust-removal system and use it.

Use something to support your workpiece while carving. Don't wedge it between your legs and go to work with a chisel. Carving-supply dealers sell a variety of clamps and vises, and we'll show you in chapter 3 how to build an old-time shaving horse that works equally well with contemporary carvings.

Read the labels on packages containing paints, cements, epoxies, solvents, and other chemicals. Some compounds should not be breathed or handled with bare skin. Be aware of the recommended precautions.

One Final Word

Don't be too quick to invest in tools and set up shop. Your workplace should reflect your carving style, and unless you know at this point exactly what that is, then you would be well advised to let things develop slowly.

Visit other carvers and sign up for workshops. A week or weekend with a professional carver can shorten the learning process for you as well as introduce you to new equipment and new ideas. A workshop can be as brief and simple as an afternoon painting session during a carving show, or it can be an elaborate seminar with a well-known professional lasting two weeks.

If you're a beginner, go for the brief classes until you focus on the type of carving you want to do, then sign up for a protracted session with the pro of your choice. It's important to keep in mind when taking workshops that your goal should be to develop your technical skills, not to become a clone of the professional carver leading the session. Therein lie the dangers of workshops. Attend enough to learn the technical aspects of carving but work at developing your individual style.

Most professional carvers hold workshops, sometimes at their own studios, sometimes in conjunction with local colleges, arts associations, carving-supply dealers, or wildfowl art exhibitions.

Jim Sprankle has taught across the United States, Canada, and in England, and he has a teaching studio at his home in Maryland. Other leading artists such as Larry Barth, Bob Guge, Ernie Muehlmatt, Greg Woodard, and Gordon Hare also teach independently or through programs such as the Ward Museum's summer workshops in Salisbury, Maryland.

A carving workshop presents a good opportunity to learn technical skills. Here professional carver Rich Smoker, right, conducts a class at the P. C. English Company.

The carving-supply company P. C. English, Inc., in Thornburg, Virginia, offers workshops with leading carvers such as Rich Smoker, who has been a regular in the P. C. English program.

The value of a workshop comes from matching your goals and needs with the skills of a particular teacher. If you're interested in carving decorative waterfowl, then a week with Jim Sprankle would be a good choice. If you want to do miniature songbirds, then find a professional who specializes in that genre, such as Bob Guge or Ernie Muehlmatt.

Don't sign up for a workshop just to say you've spent a week studying with a famous carver. Decide what you want to accomplish in your art, search out a professional you feel best equipped to help you, and then go to work.

2

Wood: How to Pick the Right Material for Your Carving

Modern bird carvers have a bewildering variety of woods from which to choose. Should you work with basswood, tupelo, eastern white cedar, paulownia, sugar pine, white pine, or some more exotic species?

The answer depends upon what kind of carving you intend to do—decorative songbird, hunting decoy, interpretive carving, and so forth—and what you want to accomplish. For example, you wouldn't select the same wood for a highly detailed carving of a bluebird as you would for a duck decoy intended to see action on the water.

In this chapter we'll discuss in general terms the most prevalent carving woods used today, and we'll help you select the proper wood for your particular carving project.

What's Best Is What's Available

Carvers are very fortunate these days because good carving wood is readily available. Even if you live in a treeless desert, stocking up with basswood and tupelo is as easy as getting out your credit card and dialing a toll-free phone number. Most carving-supply dealers carry not only a wide variety of tools but carving wood as well.

It hasn't always been so. Old-time decoy makers used what was available and what was cheap. For this reason the wood used in old decoys reflects the region in which they were made. Louisiana decoys were made of cypress root or tupelo. Eastern white cedar was used on the east coast, sugar pine in the west.

Turn-of-the-century carvers certainly had their favorite woods, but those favorites were governed by the choices available regionally and modified by materials that might show up serendipitously.

Nathan Cobb was a celebrated decoy maker whose family ran a sportsman's retreat on a Virginia barrier island in the late 1800s. When the Cobbs weren't entertaining guests, they salvaged ships that went aground on the shoals near their island. Ever-resourceful Nathan discovered that the masts of wrecked sailing ships made fine decoy wood. Nathan used the masts for bodies, and he carved heads from holly and other local woods.

Many old-time decoy makers used tree roots and limbs to make heads. They would find a piece of wood that resembled a duck or shorebird head and with a minimum of whittling would put it to use. The term "root head" is used to describe these decoys, and some contemporary carvers still practice the root-head art.

The late Steve and Lem Ward of Crisfield, Maryland, were two of America's best-known bird carvers, turning out thousands of decoys and decorative carvings over a half-century beginning in the 1920s. Their work today brings several thousand dollars per carving, but during their carving lives the brothers made a meager living at their art, supplementing their incomes by barbering.

The Wards used what was available and cheap. They made numerous decoys of balsa wood, not because balsa is a highly regarded material for wood carving, but because they once got a great deal on government-surplus life rafts made of balsa. The rafts kept their woodshed filled for some time.

I was in Louisiana recently visiting champion carver Tan Brunet, and he showed me some beautiful old gunning decoys carved by Cadis and Odee Vizier, who were market gunners in Bayou Lafourche in the days when that practice was legal. The decoys were mainly dabbling ducks—teal and pintails mostly—and they were surprisingly light and a bit smaller and more streamlined than what I was used to.

They were made of cypress root, Tan said, which was, and still is, a favorite material for gunning decoys in the bayou. The light weight of cypress makes the decoys easily portable when the hunter has to walk across wide marshes, and it is virtually rot proof. It will last forever.

The size of the decoys, however, was often determined by the size of the root available. Thus the tiny little teal and the streamlined pintails.

Many contemporary carvers prefer to work with local wood or found wood even though a wide variety of materials is available through carving suppliers. I have a stylized mallard made by British carver Guy Taplin, who works in the tradition of Nathan Cobb, using wood that washes up on the beach near his cottage on the North Sea. The mallard is made from a treated post, and even though it's about four years old, you can still get a whiff of the creosote. I don't worry about that bird rotting.

Wood for Decoy Carving

While makers of decorative birds need to concern themselves with how wood responds to the knife and to applications of paint, the decoy carver must also consider function. The decoy must float properly, must be resistant to rot, and must be sturdy enough to withstand the kind of abuse dished out on hunting trips.

Not surprisingly, many modern carvers use the same stuff the old-timers used. Grayson Chesser, the Virginia carver of traditional hunting decoys, uses eastern white cedar, as do many of his contemporaries. The decoy makers of a century ago liked the qualities of white cedar, and with good reason. It floated well, it carved easily if you could avoid pieces with knots, and it was tough. The only problem is, a century ago it was readily available, but that's not so today. A few small mills, principally in North Carolina, still offer it, but it's hard to find in the broader commercial market.

According to Grayson, the key to selecting good white cedar is to go to the mill and pick it out yourself. Mill operators don't necessarily know the qualities needed by decoy carvers.

"The best wood is sawn lengthwise into quarter sections, but it's hard to find cedar large enough to do that these days," he says. "Check the grain carefully and avoid wood that has hard, shiny veins of sap. It is very brittle, and paint won't adhere because of the sap. Likewise, avoid wood that has the dark heart string from the center of the tree. It will crack. Avoid knotty wood, although a few small knots are okay. Usually you can fit a decoy pattern between knots, unless you're doing a very large bird."

Tupelo is the material of choice in the southeastern United States, and in recent years its popularity has spread, especially among carvers of decorative birds. We'll discuss this wood in depth in the section on woods for decorative carving.

Many beginners assume that balsa would be a good carving wood, especially for gunning decoys. It's lightweight, carves easily, and is readily available. But there are drawbacks. The wood is actually too soft and light. The open pores make it difficult to paint, the fibers tend to tear when cut with a knife, and its fragility is a liability in hunting situations.

One of the most popular materials for working decoys over the past century has been cork. Cork is lightweight, easy to carve, and floats very "ducklike" according to waterfowl hunters. High-density cork is rugged and, when sealed, accepts paint readily. Indeed, many hunters don't paint their decoys at all. To create a black duck decoy, they simply heat the cork with a torch until it's a deep brown. Purists will add the purple speculum.

While cork will not stand the degree of abuse white cedar will, it can be toughened by adding a plywood bottom and a coat of sealer. Grayson Chesser uses a liquid sealer such as Val Oil, to which is added cork dust saved from cutting out the body. Rich Smoker prefers Bondo, the plastic filler body shops use to repair dents in cars. Filler and plywood bottoms do, however, add to the weight of the decoys.

Cottonwood, which is closely related to an Oriental tree called paulownia, is popular among east-coast carvers but is not widely available from commercial suppliers. Most carvers locate and cut their own or learn of sources from other carvers.

The paulownia has wide leaves and pecan-sized seed balls, and sports a bright purple flower in spring. The wood is in high demand in Japan, where they use it to make furniture, musical instruments, and veneer.

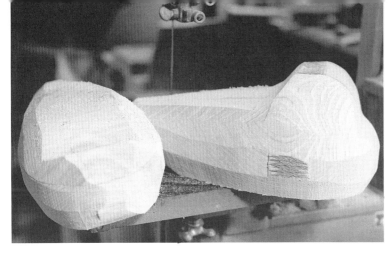

Roughed-out bodies of eastern white cedar, left, and paulownia. An advantage of paulownia is that it is light in weight and need not be hollowed out when making hunting decoys.

Waterfowl hunters say that cork is a good material for making working decoys because it floats like a duck. Wood should be used for the head and tail and can also be used as a base. This plywood tail will be cut out on the bandsaw and fitted into a notch in the cork.

The wooden tail adds strength, which is especially important if the decoys will be used in a hunting situation. This decoy, made by Grayson Chesser, will become part of his hunting rig.

A cork wood duck with head and tail added. Natural cork is too porous to accept paint well, so the surface should be sealed.

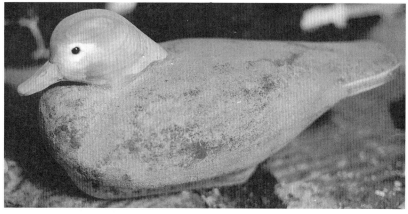

Grayson seals the cork with Val Oil, to which is added cork dust. The surface will be sanded smooth, then painted.

Cottonwood appeals to decoy carvers because it is lightweight and decoys made with it don't have to be hollowed out. The wood resists checking and splitting, is rot resistant, and is easy to carve. The trees grow fast and have wide growth rings. The wood is rough and doesn't sand well, but that's not a drawback when making hunting decoys. Indeed, a little texture avoids an unnatural glossy look.

One of the problems with cottonwood is finding a source of good quality. Trees that are large enough for carving often have had their centers eaten away by insects. If the insect tunnel is small, the wood can still be used by planing it to create a flat surface.

Cottonwood logs should be cut to length, then split, and a decoy body can be made from each side of the block. Many carvers prefer to carve it "wet" rather than allowing it to season.

Cottonwood is most often found growing in old house lots. Its fast-growth characteristics made it an appealing shade tree early in this century. The large seed pods are said to have been used for packing when goods were shipped to the United States from the Orient, and that practice helped introduce the tree to this country.

Wood for Decorative Carving

Phil English, who operates P. C. English, Inc., was a wood technology major at North Carolina State University. For someone who carves and sells carving material, that's a good choice for an academic field.

Phil English with a supply of carving wood. Tupelo, in the foreground, shows the tapered butt swell from which the carving wood is taken. The stacks in the background are basswood.

Phil's business is literally centered around wood. A large kiln is situated behind his warehouse, a shed holds thousands of board feet of basswood and tupelo, and his showroom is filled with chisels and gouges, knives, electronic cutting tools, burning tools, and various other devices designed to transform what once was a living tree into a reasonable resemblance of a living bird.

His advice to beginning carvers: Buy basswood. "Basswood is absolutely predictable," says Phil. "If it's somewhat orange in color, it will be a little hard. If it's lighter, it will be softer. You can buy it by grade and know exactly what you're getting."

Basswood is the favorite of the carver of decoratives, followed closely by tupelo, then distantly by white pine and sugar pine. Basswood is a favorite of retail dealers such as Phil and his competitors because it is readily available and is utterly predictable. The customer knows what he's getting, and Phil doesn't have to worry about returns or unhappy customers.

He buys it by the truckload, puts it in the kiln to season for two months or so, then sells it through his mail-order operation, at carving shows around the country, or in his showroom off Interstate 95 south of Fredericksburg, Virginia.

Seasoning the wood is an important part of the process. "If you intend to glue wood, the magic number is twelve percent moisture," he says. "More than twelve percent and there's a good chance the glue joint will come apart. We use a moisture meter and take the moisture content down to at least ten percent before we remove the wood from the kiln."

Other than its appeal to retailers, what makes basswood a good carving wood? It is dense, clean, and virtually without grain; the quality is consistent from block to block; and the wood is easy to carve and can be detailed with a pyrographic pen. And it accepts paint nicely.

What about some of the decoy woods mentioned earlier? A wood that is desirable for decoy making is often not suitable for decorative birds. Cottonwood, for example, is soft, loose grained, and rough textured. Those qualities are desirable in gunning-decoy material but not for decoratives. Cottonwood will not accept fine detail such as tiny feather barbs, and its texture makes it difficult to paint, especially if you use thin washes of acrylics.

White cedar and the pines tend to have knots and a pronounced grain pattern. The yellow grain is hard and dense and will not accept paint easily, while the soft, so-called summer grain soaks up paint easily. As a result, the grain pattern often shows through, and this is a liability when carving highly realistic birds.

Pines also tend to have small pockets of pitch embedded in the fibers, and these will inevitably bleed through. If pine is cured in a heated kiln, the pitch can be crystallized, but there still is no guarantee that some resin won't bleed through the paint eventually.

So we're back to basswood and to another valuable material mentioned earlier, tupelo. Louisiana carvers have won so many awards in the last ten years carving with tupelo, its popularity has spread across the country. Tupelo is the blackened redfish of the carving world.

This wood tends to be more popular among carvers than among carving-supply dealers. Both basswood and tupelo are excellent for carving, but basswood is more consistent and predictable, making it highly popular among people who buy and sell it. Tupelo can be a bit capricious.

"One tree will have great carving wood and the tree next to it will be bad," says Phil English. "Then a third tree will have some good wood in it and some bad wood. But good tupelo makes great carving wood. Basswood gets a little fuzz on it when you grind it, but tupelo doesn't. Tupelo takes detail really well and responds well to the burning tool."

The primary sources for tupelo are the freshwater swamps of Louisiana. The tree grows in flooded bottomlands, and its name is said to have come from the Creek Indians, who called it *eto,* meaning tree, and *opelwv,* meaning swamp.

The carving wood does not come from the entire tupelo tree but just from an area wide in circumference near the base called the butt swell. Usually, the trees are harvested, then the butt swell is taken for carving purposes. The smaller diameter upper portions of the tree are used primarily as corewood in furniture making. The wood is white, featureless, strong, and stable. Your cherry table is most likely made of tupelo topped with a veneer of cherry.

The big butt swell of tupelo, however, has shown up in hundreds of award-winning bird carvings in recent years. Many carvers prefer tupelo over all other wood, including basswood.

The only problem is inconsistency, and this is why Phil English advises beginning carvers to opt for the predictability of basswood. Once you get your feet on the ground as a carver, then you can experiment, he says.

Tupelo comes in short lengths and sometimes odd sizes, which makes it unappealing to commercial dealers. It is sold mainly by small mills that buy stump rights after a tupelo crop is harvested. Go to a carving show and you'll see a dozen entrepreneurs in the parking lot selling tupelo out of their pickup trucks.

Exotica

The woods we've discussed so far are valuable to carvers because of the way they respond to the cutting edge, their ability to accept paint, and, in the case of hunting decoys, their toughness and tendency to float in a ducklike manner. But few bird carvings actually get near the water, and many never see a wash of paint. Some carvers choose wood for its own innate characteristics.

Leo Osborne can do wonderful things with a redwood burl and some chisels and gouges. In his case the wood is not a means to an end, it is both the beginning and the end. The integrity of the wood is what is important, and he sees his role as an artist as being something of a facilitator. His goal is to find some wonderful form hidden in the wood and to bring it out for everyone to see. So Leo chooses wood with character, with a story to tell.

Likewise, wood sculptors such as Martin Gates and Dave and Mary Ahrendt work with the wood to create exciting visual forms. The Ahrendts will often paint just enough detail to make the bird identifiable, then leave the remainder to the imagination of the viewer. A particular example is their striking sculpture of a peregrine falcon attacking a pair of swifts. The heads of the birds are detailed and sharp, but the remainder is blurred, symbolizing the great speed at which the action is taking place.

Martin Gates, who lives in central Florida, often sculpts herons and other wading birds with reptiles, creating a definite Florida flavor in his work. At his home are dozens of giant stumps and blocks of various woods aging in the Florida heat. He uses walnut, mahogany, pecan, whatever is available and strikes his fancy.

John Sharp of Kent, Ohio, is a master of sculpting birds in natural wood. He will often carve an entire group of birds from a single block of walnut or other hardwood. A wonderful example would be his carving of five cormorants, which won the Ward World Championship in Interpretive Sculpture in 1991. The piece is carved from a single massive piece of walnut.

John Sharp's carving of five shags is from a single piece of walnut. The work won first place in interpretive sculpture at world level in the 1991 Ward World Championship. (Photo courtesy of the Ward Foundation.)

Choosing wood, like choosing tools, is a matter of personal taste and carving style. It depends upon what you want to accomplish, what you want to say with your carving. Some of us enjoy wood for its own qualities, its color, form, texture, patina. For others, wood is a tool, a medium to which pigment is applied, something of a three-dimensional canvas.

Leo Osborne's *Still Not Listening* depicts the dangers of an oil spill on shorebirds and was created after the 1989 *Exxon Valdez* spill in Prince William Sound. It was carved from a 26-inch-diameter maple bird's-eye burl. It won an honorable mention in the 1989 Ward competition and received the 1990 Judges' Award for environmental sculpture at the Pacific Rim Wildlife Art Show. (Photo by Benjamin Magro, courtesy of the artist.)

Leo Osborne's *Water's Edge* was carved from a redwood burl measuring 48 x 16 x 8 inches. It depicts a swallow dipping for water and won a first in interpretive at the 1989 Ward competition. (Photo by Benjamin Magro.)

The enjoyable aspect of bird carving is that all of these approaches are valid. The manner in which you use wood depends totally upon your motivation as an artist. What is it you want to show us? What do you have to say?

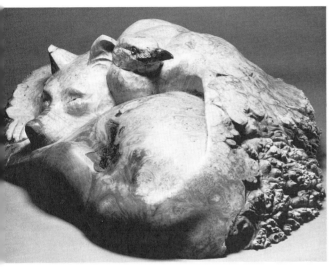

Leo Osborne's *Brothers of the Wood* depicts a wolf and raven emerging from wood, in this case a maple burl. Leo created this sculpture to depict the harmony and symbiosis of the two creatures and to demonstrate the dependence and "oneness" of nature. It won second place at world level in the 1991 Ward competition and won best in show at the 1991 Pacific Rim show in Tacoma, Washington.

The Stoop is a 1990 sculpture by Dave and Mary Ahrendt of Minnesota. The Ahrendts carved the peregrine falcon from a piece of black walnut 34 inches in height. The head of the bird is detailed and painted, but the remainder is left in natural finish, depicting the speed of the falcon.

25

Dave and Mary Ahrendt's 1991 sculpture *Soaring* depicts a golden eagle in flight. The black walnut is left undetailed and in natural finish, except for the head of the bird.

Busting the Flock shows a merlin attacking chipping sparrows in this 1991 work by the Ahrendts. It is carved from black walnut and stands 16 inches high.

Martin Gates's *Black Gold, Black Death* depicts an eagle and a skull and was carved in response to the *Exxon Valdez* oil spill.

Martin Gates carved *Fish Mongers* from pecan.

Martin Gates's *Shadow Stalker* was carved from holly.

Martin Gates carved this turtle from cherry.

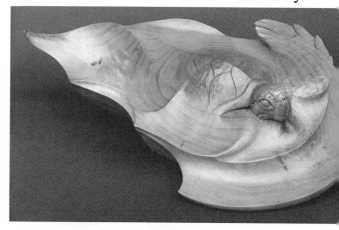

This heron was carved from cherry by Martin Gates.

3 Traditional Tools: Good Things Are Made to Last

The nice thing about bird carving is that you can make a decoy or a simply carved songbird with a minimum of tools. Sure, the catalogs have page after page of electronic grinders, detailers, and various other gizmos, but before investing in modern electronic equipment, it would be a good idea to familiarize yourself with some of the traditional tools of the carving profession. After all, power tools don't necessarily make you a better carver, just a faster carver.

On my mantel are four birds carved by a local man some forty years ago. He is long since deceased, and I know him only through stories told by people who lived in his town. He was a man of modest means who lived alone in a small house without modern conveniences. Birds were his passion and he loved to carve and paint them. His tools were as modest as his lifestyle. He worked with a pocketknife, a few small chisels and gouges, and some paintbrushes purchased at the local five-and-dime.

Understandably, his birds do not have the detail and sophistication of contemporary carvings, but they succeed in capturing something essential about the species they depict. In a very simple and uncomplicated way he could bring a block of wood to life. A yellowlegs is preening feathers along its back; a Canada goose is holding a branch in its bill; a magnolia warbler is perched on a tree branch.

The old man had no burning tools or grinders to add feather detail to the warbler, so he used an ice pick or some such sharp instrument to scribe shallow lines that suggest feather detail. The wings are carefully carved, and the tail feathers are made to overlay each other, creating a nice impression of texture and depth.

To some observers these old carvings appear crude, but in my mind they show what can be done with rudimentary tools, some imagination and determination, and a love of wild birds.

Perhaps if all bird carvers started with just a knife or two and a few chisels and gouges, they would better appreciate that the goal in bird carving is not to see how many feathers you can replicate but to capture the essence of a certain species of bird.

The Basics

Old-time decoy makers got by with just a few basic tools: a hatchet, knife, rasp, two or three sizes of gouges, and a drawknife for rounding the body. Many contemporary carvers turn out beautiful birds using these same, time-tested tools.

One of the best makers of working decoys in America today is Jimmie Vizier of Galliano, Louisiana. If an ability to carve birds can be passed on by genetic code, then certainly this man of Louisiana's Bayou Lafourche has inherited a wealth of talent. Jimmie's father, Odee Vizier, and his uncle, Cadis Vizier, were legendary Louisiana decoy makers and market hunters of the early 1900s. Jimmie learned from them, carving working decoys as a young boy growing up in Galliano.

In the old-time tradition of the Cajun carvers, Jimmie uses the hatchet extensively in roughing out and shaping his decoys. The old-time Cajun carvers, like many of the previous generation of decoy makers, were artists with this simple tool. "When my father and his brother finished working with the hatchet, there wasn't much left to do with the pocketknife," Jimmie says. "The hatchets they used were smaller than the ones we have today, and they were kept razor sharp. They made thousands of decoys, and in time they got to where they could do some very fine work. Their ability to handle a hatchet was amazing."

The same can be said of Jimmie. Few think of the hatchet as a precision cutting instrument, but in the hands of a master carver like Jimmie, each cut is exact, and within just a few minutes he can have a decoy body roughed out. He creates the contours of the body and head with a Foredom flexible-shaft cutter. After

World-champion carver Tan Brunet of Galliano, Louisiana, is noted for his meticulously finished decorative decoys, but he begins each carving in the old Cajun tradition, with a small hatchet or adz. Here he works on the chopping block while his son Jett works on a project of his own in the background. Note that Tan is carving the head and body as one instead of carving the head separately and attaching it to the body.

Tan uses a minimum of tools to rough out the decoy: hatchet, rasp, knife, and a small hand router, a knife with a circular blade handy for shaping the cheek area of the head.

rounding off the body and head, Jimmie uses the knife to carve the bill, the head, and body detail.

Decoy maker Grayson Chesser, like Jimmie Vizier, prefers traditional tools, especially when making an item as tradition bound as the decoy. Grayson's only power tools are a bandsaw, which is used for roughing out bodies and heads, and a drill press, which speeds things up when he hollows out a decoy.

Grayson's collection of hand tools is rather modest. Once a decoy is roughed out on the bandsaw, Grayson shapes it with a hand-held rasp, a spokeshave, and a knife. "You can get by with those three tools," he says. "Buy a good quality general-purpose carving knife, such as a Knotts number six, a spokeshave, and a half-round rasp. Once you get the feel for what these tools can do, then you might want to add some additional ones."

The spokeshave is a wood plane designed to cut contours; Grayson uses it to round out the body and head. Then the rasp refines the job, removing any flat spots left by the spokeshave blade. Sandpaper removes the rasp marks. The carving knife is used to shape the head and to add detail to the body, such as overlapping wingtips and tail feathers.

Grayson also uses a small knife (a Knotts number 4) for carving fine detail, a drawknife, an X-acto hand router, a Sur-form shaper, and a small handsaw.

The drawknife is similar to the spokeshave, but the latter has adjustable blade depth, like a plane. The hand router has a small, circular blade that is handy for cutting contours, such as the cheek line on the head of a decoy. It is similar to a scorp, a tool used for roughing out bowls, spoons, and other concave shapes.

The Sur-form shaper is something of a cross between a rasp and a plane. It has a rasplike blade, with handles like a plane. It's good for working under the tail and in other spots that a half-round rasp won't reach. The handsaw is used for shaping the wingtips.

Chisels and Gouges

Carving-supply stores have an almost limitless variety of chisels and gouges. They come in many sizes and shapes and are handy for a variety of bird-carving projects. Martin Gates of Micanopy, Florida, a world-champion carver working in the unpainted, so-called interpretive style, uses chisels and gouges almost exclusively once a workpiece is roughed out with a chain saw or bandsaw.

Marty's hobby is collecting antique tools, and many of the chisels and gouges he uses on a daily basis are collector's items. He enjoys the deliberate pace, the precision, and the quiet, dust-free working environment provided by chisels and gouges. (See the Bird Carving Basics volumes *Heads* and *Bills and Beaks* for details on Marty's carving methods.)

If you want to try carving with hand tools such as these, begin with just a chisel and a few gouges and buy the best quality you can afford. A good tool will last a lifetime if it is properly cared for and will be a pleasure to use.

It's easy to become intimidated if you scan the offerings of gouges in tool catalogs. They come in an amazing variety of sizes and shapes. If you're going to pick out just six tools to begin with, how do you know which ones to select?

First, let's consider shapes and sizes. A carver's chisel has a straight cutting surface, while the cutting surface of a gouge is curved. The carver's chisel is similar to a carpenter's chisel, but the cutting edge of the carver's chisel is beveled on both sides. The carpenter's chisel is beveled on only one.

A gouge is categorized by two factors: size and sweep. Size refers to the width of the cutting edge and is usually measured in millimeters. Sweep refers to the degree of curvature of the blade and is indicated by a number.

A carver's chisel has no sweep at all and is referred to as a number 1 chisel. A number 2 gouge has a slight curvature; a number 9 gouge is deeply curved, almost in a U shape. A gouge with number 11 sweep is distinctly U shaped and is called a veiner, while a blade with a V shape is called a parting tool.

The size and shape of the tool you select depends upon the job you want to do. A large number 9 gouge would be used for scooping out a great deal of wood, while a tool with a shallow sweep would be used to remove very thin layers. Veining tools and parting tools are used to add detail and relief.

Beyond a consideration of size and sweep, there is also a question of blade shape when purchasing gouges. Standard tools have straight, gently tapering blades, and these are good for most tasks. But there will come a time in a carving project when a straight blade simply will not work, such as when carving detail in a recessed area. Then, too, there will be areas on a carving where the standard broad blade cannot be used without endangering nearby detail.

Chisels and gouges have been used for centuries, and any problem you face will inevitably have been faced before and tool makers will have come up with a tool to solve the problem.

The fishtail gouge, for example, tapers back quickly from the cutting edge and is handy for getting into tight areas without doing damage to surrounding detail.

Some gouges are bent, or offset, making it easier to scoop wood out of recessed areas. Spoon gouges are cupped like a common tablespoon and can be worked in areas a straight blade cannot. Back-bent gouges have the curve of the blade reversed, so the cutting edge is convex instead of concave. These are used to get a clean cut where top clearance is limited. A skew is a chisel with an angled cutting edge, handy for removing wood from tight corners.

So, now that you're going to pick out a set of six tools to begin your sculpting career, where do you begin?

Fortunately, most carving-supply dealers offer kits with a half-dozen very useful tools. Many beginners buy a modest kit to get started, then add other tools when specific needs arise. Again, buy the best quality you can afford. If you must skimp, skimp on the number of tools instead of on quality.

The Woodcraft catalog (see Appendix for address and phone), for example, offers a high-quality Swiss Sculptor's Set, which includes six tools, a 24-ounce lignum vitae mallet, and a canvas tool roll. Included are the following: 30-mm chisel, 30-mm skew, 30-mm no. 5 gouge, 30-mm no. 7 bent gouge, 35-mm no. 9 gouge, and 20-mm no. 12 parting tool. At this writing, the set was selling for around $180.

Staying Sharp

If you stop by Martin Gates's studio and watch him work for a few hours, you'll notice that he makes frequent trips to the polishing wheel to strop a chisel or a gouge. It is imperative to use sharp cutting tools, whether they are chisels, gouges, hatchets, spokeshaves, knives, or chain saws. A sharp tool is a pleasure to use; a dull tool is frustrating at best, uncontrollable and dangerous at worst.

It's important to learn how to sharpen your tools and to take the time to do it regularly. Generally, most methods of sharpening call for using a stone to put the proper angle on a blade, then using a polishing wheel with rouge or an oiled leather strop to hone the blade to razor sharpness.

"The time you spend sharpening tools will be some of the most productive time you spend in your shop," says Grayson Chesser. "If you spend a day carving, you'll need to sharpen your tools before you start back again. The secret is to keep your cutting tools sharp at all times. If they get too dull, it's very hard to get a good edge on them again. If your blade tears the wood instead of cutting it, you know it's time to resharpen."

Sharpening techniques vary from carver to carver. Blacksmith and knife maker Jack Andrews, writing in the fall 1991 edition of the Ward Foundation's *Wildfowl Art Journal,* recommends using three textures of sharpening stones (course, medium, fine) and honing oil to flush away particles of metal being removed from the blade. Jack recommends dressing the blade using the three stones in coarse-to-fine order, then stropping to remove burr and to develop a keen edge. The coarse stone is used only if a blade is extremely dull, he says.

The strop is the carver's most important sharpening tool, Jack says. He recommends making one by attaching to a board a piece of belt leather at least two by eight inches. The leather should be lightly coated with honing oil and dusted with 400- to 600-grit aluminum oxide powder. The strop should be kept at your work area so you can touch up blades as needed.

Carving-supply dealers offer a wide variety of sharpening aids. Bruce Burk recommends in *Game Bird Carving* the Lansky Sharpening System, which consists of a clamp to hold the knife blade and a guide to hold the sharpening stone at a proper angle to the blade. Bruce recommends an angle of twenty-five degrees for carving knives. The blade should be stropped on leather or on a power stropping wheel to remove burr and gain a keen edge.

No matter what method of sharpening you use, it's important to keep your blades sharp at all times.

Make tool sharpening a part of your daily carving routine; don't allow yourself to consider it a chore. Have patience, advises Jack Andrews.

Carver Mark McNair of Virginia's Eastern Shore uses tool sharpening as part of his creative process. "Some mornings I'll go out to the shop and I'm just not motivated, the juices aren't flowing," he says. "So I spend some time straightening up my work area and sharpening my tools. Sharpening my knives puts me in the groove. It's part of the ritual of preparing to carve birds."

The Shaving Horse

Once you've assembled your tools, sharpened your blades, and decided on a carving project, you'll need something to hold your workpiece. Some carvers temporarily attach a wooden keel to a decoy and use this keel to mount the bird in a vise while working on it. Carving-supply stores offer various vises and clamps designed to hold a workpiece steady while you work with knives and chisels. The importance of such a device will become painfully apparent to you the first time a blade slips from the workpiece and makes contact with your arm or leg. Always have your workpiece firmly supported—it's easier to work on and infinitely safer.

One of the more venerable methods of holding a workpiece is called the shaving horse. It was used by old-time decoy makers, who borrowed the design from furniture makers and related craftsmen. The classic shaving horse is a simple design, very efficient, and easy to make. Carver Pete Peterson of Northampton County, Virginia, has used one for years, and he furnished the diagram illustrated here to guide you in making your own.

"The concept of the shaving horse is as old as the drawknife," says Pete. "Craftsmen have been using variations of the design for centuries, and it works equally well today."

The purpose of the shaving horse is to hold a piece of wood while you shape it. The shaving horse consists of a bench, a working surface, and a wooden clamp held firmly by foot pressure. The shaving horse is especially designed to work with the drawknife because the grip on the workpiece tightens as you pull with the knife and push with your legs. It will hold heads as well as decoy bodies of different sizes and can also be used with chisels and knives.

"I got this design from Wendell Sheerman," Pete relates. "He was an apprentice furniture maker when he was a young man growing up in Missouri, and that might be where he came up with it. He used to make miniature carvings of decoy shops, and I saw the shaving horse in one of them and decided to make a full-sized model for my own use. I've been using one for twenty-one years to carve hunting decoys. It's easy to make and can be adapted to various uses. The dimensions shown are of my own shaving horse, which is built for my comfort and convenience. People who are taller or shorter (Pete is about six feet tall) might want to alter the measurements somewhat."

Almost any kind of lumber can be used. Pete used driftwood picked up on the beach near his home, but he recommends using a hardwood such as hickory or oak for the top of the clamp because it is under a great deal of pressure when being used.

Wooden Horseshoes and Brush Racks

Pete has adapted several designs from old-time decoy makers to his shop. A holder he calls a wooden horseshoe is used with the spokeshave when working on decoy bodies. Pete got the idea from Charlie Joiner, a decoy maker from Maryland's Eastern Shore.

Joiner also taught Pete to use a plane in a vise to flatten the area of the body where the head will attach. The vise is firmly clamped in, blade up, and the wood is moved over the surface of the plane instead of vice versa. The technique creates a perfectly flat mounting area, ensuring a tight fit of the head to the body.

Another Charlie Joiner contribution to Pete's shop is the paintbrush holder illustrated here. It's a simple design, but one that keeps brushes at the ready. "I paint my decoys all at once, so I need to use several brushes at the same time," says Pete. "The rack helps keep them organized."

Pete does most of his carving with the drawknife and a Russell-Dexter fodder knife, designed for cutting corn fodder. Pete liked the shape of the handle and the quality of the steel, so he began using the knives for decoy carving.

Pete has his drawknives sharpened by a company that specializes in sharpening butcher knives—Norfolk Grinding and Equipment Company in Norfolk, Virginia (see Appendix). They put on the edge and Pete maintains it with a leather strop. A drawknife will last him about three months before it needs to be reground.

Sculptor's adzes have narrow blades and can be used for decoy making.

In talented hands a hatchet can do surprisingly fine work. Mark McNair shapes the bill of a wood duck here.

A bandsaw makes it quick and easy to cut out heads and bodies. Good bandsaws are expensive, though, and an alternative would be to use a handsaw such as a coping saw or jigsaw. Or you could sketch your patterns on wood, then take the blocks to a custom woodshop and have them cut out.

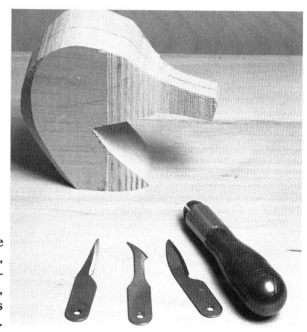

While most professional carvers use expensive custom-made knives, you could begin with a changeable-blade set like this KBL3 knife kit, which gives you three different blades at a cost of less than $20.

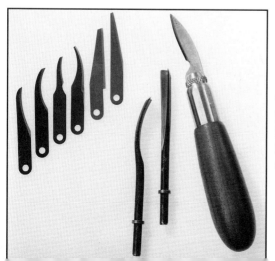

The Combi-M knife set includes a bent gouge, parting tool, whittling blade, and six blades for carving. It has a walnut handle and brass jaw and sells for around $35.

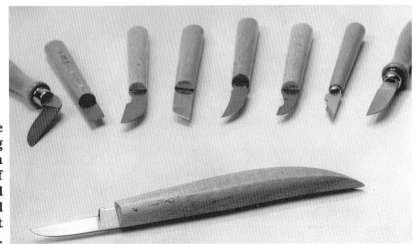

German-made Chip carving knives come in a variety of sizes and shapes and sell for about $10 each.

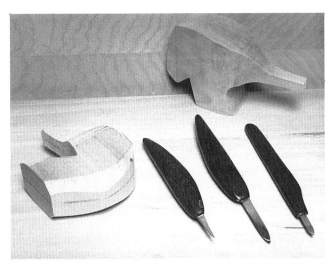

Custom knives are the choice of many carvers. These are made by Chester Knotts and his son Allan of Florida. Two detail knives flank a general-purpose carving knife. They sell for around $30 each.

A knife kit will give you a good idea of what different blade shapes will do. Here, a general-purpose blade on the KBL3 set is used to rough out a bill.

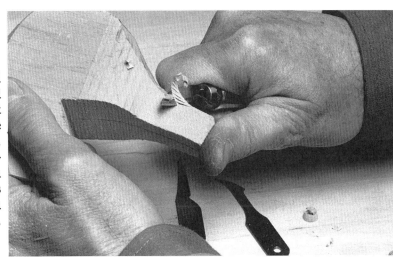

As you gain experience as a carver, you'll find several favorite blades that you'll use for different purposes. A short blade such as this is good for carving detail.

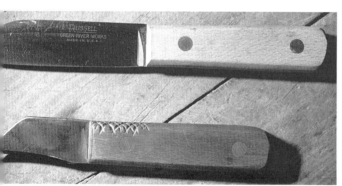

Pete Peterson's favorite knives were not designed for bird carving but for cutting corn fodder. Pete likes the large handles and the quality of steel in the blades, which enables them to maintain a sharp edge. Pete shortened the blade on the bottom knife and added a crosshatch pattern on the handle to improve the grip.

Wood rasps have long been used by carvers to shape hunting decoys. A rasp will remove a surprising amount of wood and will remove flat spots left by a spokeshave or drawknife. The old-time decoy makers sometimes left the rasp marks on their birds to give a textured look.

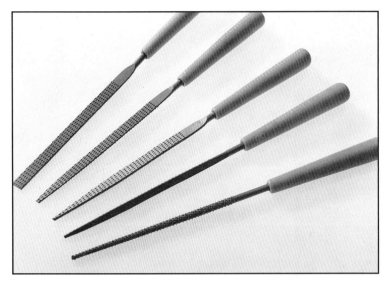

Rasps come in a variety of shapes and sizes: flat, half-round, triangular, round, and so forth. For decoy carving the half-round is handy because it has a flat surface on one side and a convex surface on the other, which is good for curved areas such as the neck and head.

A drawknife is like a plane without the depth adjustment. It is pulled along the surface of the wood in the direction of the grain, and the amount of wood removed is determined by the angle at which the blade is held to the workpiece.

Jimmie Vizier of Galliano, Louisiana, was schooled by his father and uncle in the Cajun tradition of decoy making—using hatchets, knives, and chisels—and he still works in that tradition, using some modern tools to speed up the carving process. Here he traces a pattern on a block of tupelo.

Like the old-time carvers, Jimmie uses a small hatchet to round off the body after cutting it out on a bandsaw.

The head and body are roughed out separately, then the head will be attached before the final carving process begins.

To refine the shape of the decoy, Jimmie uses a carbide bit on his Foredom tool, a flexible-shaft grinder capable of turning up to 18,000 rpm. As the flying wood chips indicate, a Foredom will remove wood in a hurry.

The Foredom tool consists of a motor in a housing designed to be hung from the workbench or shelf. It's attached by a flexible shaft to a hand piece that will accept a variety of abrasives.

With a carbide bit locked in the hand piece, Jimmie quickly rounds off the head and bill.

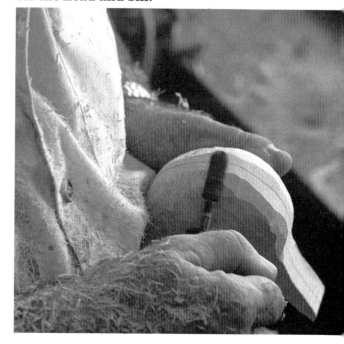

The bill is shaped with a knife, then the head is attached to the body with two-part epoxy cement.

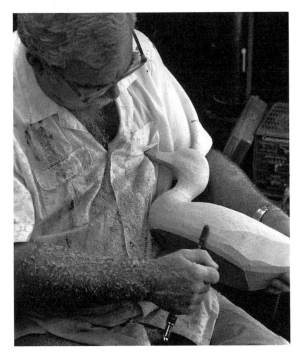

With the cement dry, Jimmie uses the Foredom again to further refine the shape.

By attaching the head at this stage in the carving process, Jimmie can use the Foredom to shape the breast and neck, creating a graceful curve.

The pintail is beginning to take shape. Jimmie frequently checks the bird for symmetry.

The body is rounded off, then the Foredom is used to carve the separation of the wings along the back.

Old-time carvers sometimes used a rifle-bullet casing with a sharpened edge to cut holes in which to insert glass eyes. This tool is a refinement of the old idea—a brass tube attached to a wooden handle.

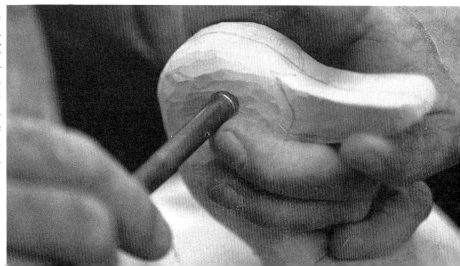

This is the Foredom tool, showing the motor housing, shaft, and hand piece. A set of cutters in a plastic case accompanies the tool.

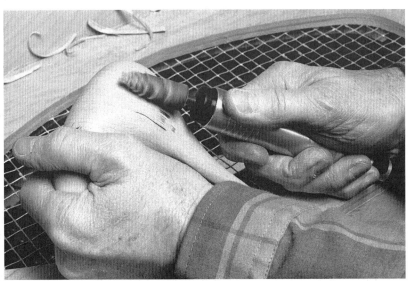

The Foredom can be used for sanding when this special attachment is used. The motor is activated by a foot pedal, leaving the hands free to hold the workpiece.

A lineup of Karbide Kutzall bits shows the variety of shapes and sizes that can be used with a flexible-shaft machine such as the Foredom.

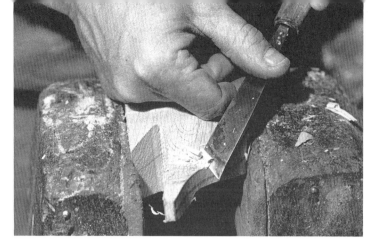

A variety of chisels and gouges are used in bird carving. This skew chisel (it has an angled cutting surface) is used to shape the head and bill of a wood duck.

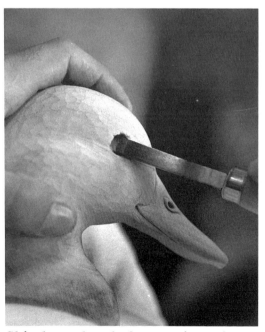

Chisels are handy for a variety of reasons. Here, Jett Brunet uses one to remove wood from an eye socket. The socket had been cut with a sharpened brass tube, and the waste wood is flicked out with the chisel.

A chisel is being used here by carver Mark McNair, but a general-purpose knife, a half-round rasp, or a flexible-shaft power tool could be used as well. As you gain experience as a carver, you'll develop favorite tools for specific purposes.

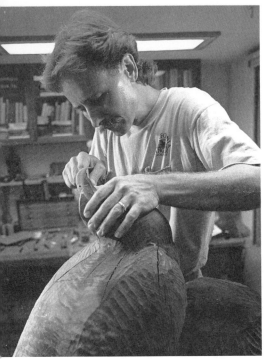

Martin is a tool collector and owns dozens of chisels and gouges in myriad shapes and sizes. This is a fishtail gouge, designed for removing wood from a broad area. The key to working with these tools is to keep them extremely sharp and to have your workpiece supported firmly.

Artist Martin Gates of Micanopy, Florida, is a master with the chisel and gouge. Martin roughs out his work with power tools, but hand tools are used from there on. He likes the quiet, the freedom from dust, and the degree of control provided by high-quality chisels and gouges.

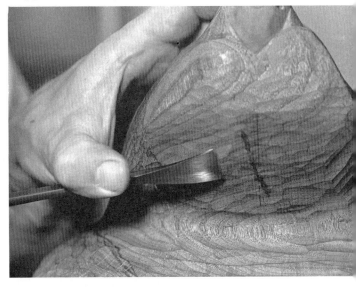

With this gouge Martin is able to shave tiny slices of walnut from the sculpture of the eagle he is working on. If you want to try working with chisels and gouges, invest in a good starter set of six tools. A good quality set will cost about $100 to $200.

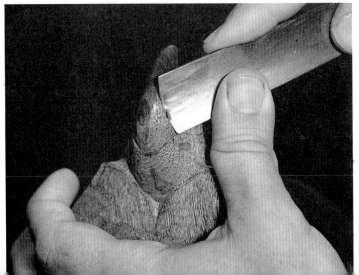

50

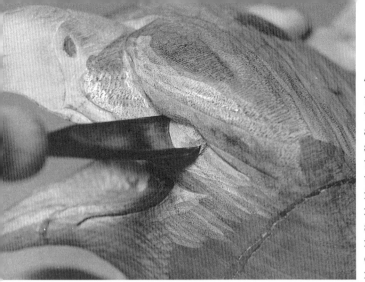

This number 9 gouge has just the right sweep for cutting the eye of the eagle. Gouges are classed according to sweep (the degree of curvature) and size (the width of the cutting edge measured in inches or millimeters). A number 2 gouge has a very slight curvature, while a number 9 is deeply curved. A chisel, number 1 sweep, has no curvature at all.

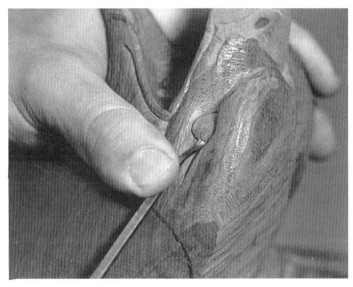

Once the outline of the eye has been cut, Martin makes the eyeball appear convex by cutting away material from outside the eye, then curving the eyeball itself. This small spoon gouge is perfect for that task. The spoon gouge has an offset cutting surface and is used where a long, straight blade would be impractical.

Chisels and gouges raise the fibers of the wood somewhat. Martin uses a burnishing tool to compress the wood after cutting.

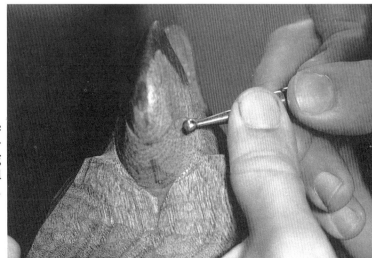

Knives are safer and more efficient to use when they are sharp. A stone is used to put an edge on a blade, then a strop is used to remove burr and produce a keen edge. A strop can be made with a piece of oiled belt leather, or you can use a power-strop attachment with an electric drill, as shown here.

The shaving horse is an ancient design but eminently usable today. These are the dimensions of Pete Peterson's shaving horse; you can make yours larger or smaller to tailor to your needs. Pine lumber can be used, with the exception of the top of the clamp, which should be hardwood. Anchoring the shaving horse to a workbench or wall will make it more stable.

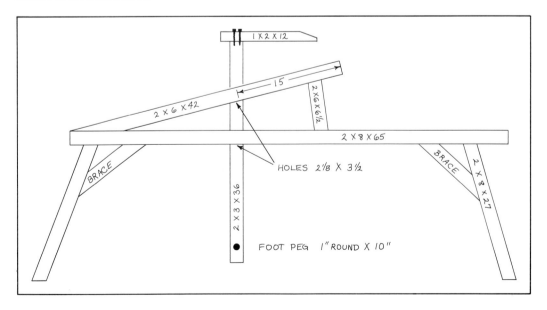

1 X 2 X 12

15

2 X 6 X 42

2 X 6 X 6½

2 X 8 X 65

BRACE

BRACE

2 X 8 X 27

HOLES 2⅛ X 3½

2 X 3 X 36

FOOT PEG 1" ROUND X 10"

Pete at work on his shaving horse. The design works well with a drawknife. Pete places his feet on the foot pegs, then pulls the drawknife toward him. As he pulls with his arms while pushing with his legs, the clamp holds the workpiece increasingly tighter.

A close-up shows how the clamp holds the workpiece in place. The angled shelf holds the carving at a comfortable working height, and the plywood base with dowels helps keep the workpiece from swiveling.

Body motion when using the drawknife with the shaving horse is similar to rowing a boat. You pull back with your arms while pushing with your legs. Pressure on the foot pegs keeps the clamp firmly pressed upon the workpiece.

The drawknife is like a plane without depth-of-cut adjustments. You need to use both hands when using it, thus the importance of the shaving horse or some other method of anchoring the workpiece.

A drawknife should always be used with the beveled side down, as shown. The tool rides along the edge of the bevel, and depth of cut is determined by the angle at which the knife is pulled.

While the shaving horse is handy for holding decoy bodies, it also can be used to hold smaller items, such as this head. A block is used under the head to raise it to comfortable working height.

The shaving horse is not used exclusively with the drawknife. Here Pete uses a chisel to carve a decoy body.

A little gizmo Pete calls a wooden horseshoe is used to hold a decoy body while shaping it with the spokeshave. The spokeshave is similar to the drawknife, but the depth of cut is adjusted as with a plane.

The wooden horseshoe, another tool of the old-time carvers, anchors the body while Pete shapes it. The horseshoe is attached to the end of Pete's workbench. The center slot is designed to hold the front of the decoy, while the grooves are designed to hold the tail.

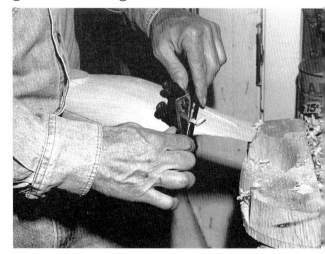

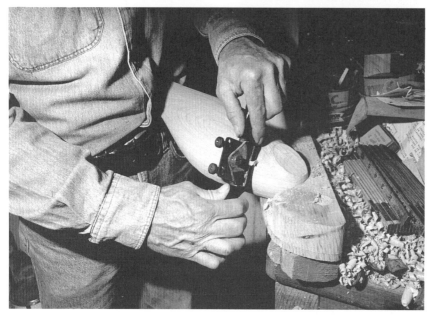

The horseshoe holds the body at almost any angle Pete needs as he shaves away thin layers of wood. Pete says he got the idea from Charlie Joiner, a Maryland decoy maker.

Another of Charlie Joiner's ideas is this paintbrush holder, designed to keep a variety of brushes near at hand. Pete paints his decoys all at once and needs several brushes at virtually the same time.

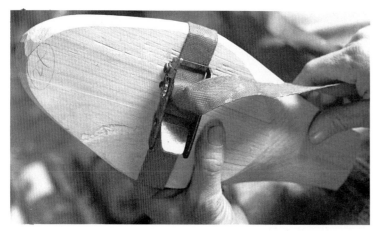

Many carvers discover handy applications for tools never intended for bird carving. This strap clamp is used to hold the body together after it has been hollowed out and glued back together. Clamps such as this are available in most hardware and building-supply stores.

When attaching the head to the body, the joining surfaces must match perfectly and should be at the proper angle. Pete solves this problem by using a plane mounted upside down in his woodworking vise. First the body, then the head are planed, ensuring a flat mating surface.

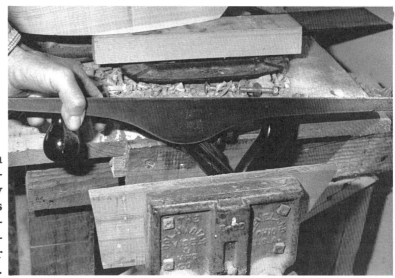

This is another idea used by old-time woodworkers and decoy makers. Bench planes such as this, with the elevated curve at midpoint, were designed for such use.

Why not put the workpiece in the vise and use the plane on it conventionally? This method produces a flatter surface because the plane is anchored at a 180-degree angle to the workpiece, ensuring a flat surface where the neck meets the head.

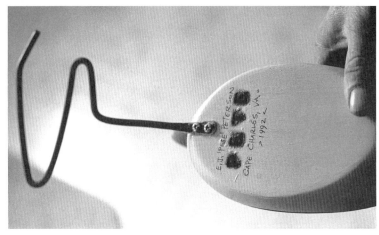

Another of Pete's home-made tools is the painting hook, or handle. The hook is attached to the decoy where the leather line loop will later go. The handle makes it easy to paint the bird, then it can be used to hang the decoy up to dry.

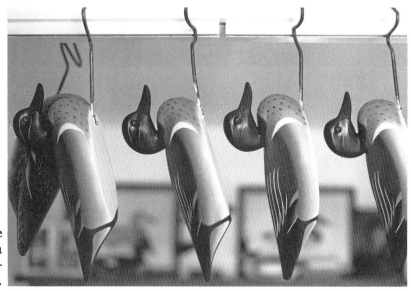

These teal were painted, then hung in a door-way to dry.

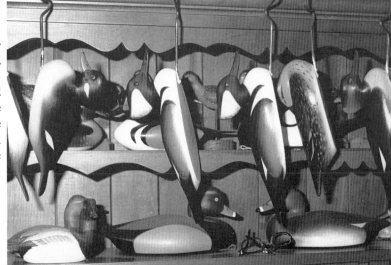

After a few days of paint-ing, Pete's home is filled with hanging decoys. Pete paints a decoy all at once, meaning that by the time he finishes, there is not a dry spot by which to hold it. So the handle is an important tool.

58

4
Tools for Decorative Carving: State of the Art and Then Some

You've just returned from a wildlife art show and now you want to give bird carving a try. You envision carving a perfect little Carolina wren perched on a pine branch or maybe even a miniature golden eagle with a field mouse in her talons. The next time you go to a carving show, you'll be an exhibitor, not just a browser. Who knows, you might even sell a few carvings. This could be the beginning of a second career.

There's an empty corner in the garage that you can convert to a carving studio, and now all you have to do is stock it with the proper tools. The professional carvers you've talked with use flexible-shaft grinders, burning tools, and a variety of bits, cutters, and stones. These are expensive, but no more so than a nice set of golf clubs. Think of it as an investment. After a few wrens and golden eagles, the tools will be paid for.

This is the point at which aspiring carvers need to sit down, take a deep breath, and lock their credit cards in a time-controlled vault. Now is not the time to go out and spend big bucks for the latest electronic carving gizmos. Sure, you're anxious to become a "famous artist," but first you need a plan.

Before you buy carving tools, consider first the kinds of carving you want to do. You have no interest in hunting, you say, and you don't want to make decoys. But you would like to carve wrens and cardinals, warblers and titmice, birds you see on your weekend hikes. You want to be able to produce intricate feather detail and a highly realistic replica of a living bird.

If such is the case, you can select from a wide variety of tools tailored for carving so-called decorative

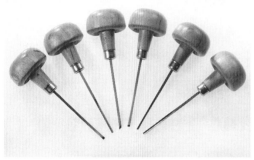

Chisels and gouges can be used for decorative carving. Micro-carving sets such as this are miniature versions of hand tools discussed in the previous chapter and are used for carving songbirds and miniatures where detail must be precise. This set includes chisels, skew, parting tool, and number 11 gouge, and comes in either 1.5 mm, 2 mm, or 3 mm.

birds. In the parlance of bird carving, a decorative bird is one simply to be looked at and admired as opposed to a bird with an obvious function, such as a hunting decoy.

There are many tools that will enable you to carve a realistic bird and to capture every barb and quill, and not all of them are powered by electricity. But before you buy, consider the type of work environment you want and evaluate your hand-eye skills and dexterity.

Generally, you can choose between old-fashioned hand tools and modern electronic carving aids such as flexible-shaft cutters and burning pens. Or you can combine the best of both worlds, using power tools for some aspects of carving and hand tools for others.

A carver's choice in tools reflects his or her tastes and abilities. For some artists carving is a quiet, reflective act, and they resent the intrusion of power tools, which can be noisy and messy, creating substantial amounts of dust, which must be removed by cumbersome (and noisy) vacuum devices. These carvers enjoy the simplicity of using hand tools—knives, chisels, gouges, and the like.

But it takes a great deal of skill and dexterity to carve a realistic bird using only hand tools, and even with the best of tools, carving can be physically demanding, perhaps even impossible for those with arthritis or other ailments. For them the power tools are a godsend.

Which should you buy—hand tools or power tools? Many carvers and suppliers recommend that you begin with hand tools because they give you a real feel for the way wood responds to a sharp edge. And, of course, they are a lot cheaper. You can get started with a knife and assorted small gouges for about $100,

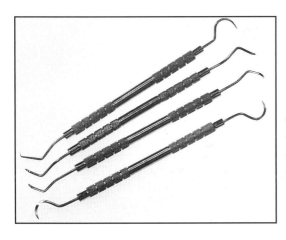

This set should be familiar to dentists. The sculpting set is ideal when extreme precision is called for, such as when shaping the membrane around a bird's eye. The set is made of stainless steel and is strong enough to sculpt wood or epoxy.

while a flexible-shaft power tool will run $200 to $700 or more.

Even most folks who sell power tools recommend that you begin with something more basic. "Hand tools will do everything a power tool will do, only slower," a spokesman with the Woodcraft Company of Parkersburg, West Virginia, told me. "We recommend that beginning carvers start with a knife, a small V-shaped tool, and some small gouges. A burning pen can be used to add feather detail. In most cases it's best to delay purchasing a flexible-shaft tool until you're sure what type of carving you want to do."

Flexible-Shaft Tools

Let's say you've tried the knives and gouges, and now you want something that will remove wood quicker and with more control. What are the advantages of the flexible-shaft tools? How much will they cost you? And what types of accessories should you buy?

Flexible-shaft cutting tools have been around for a long time. The venerable Dremel has been used by model makers for years and is still popular with carvers. But the last decade has seen a surge in popularity of more powerful and versatile cutting tools, many of which were borrowed from dental labs and engraving shops.

The advantage of the flexible-shaft tool is that it is powerful and versatile, with interchangeable bits that can remove vast quantities of wood or create subtle tufts of feathers. Some tools are more powerful than others, some are more compact, and some are more versatile.

Phil English of the P. C. English Company says the Foredom tool is a good value for beginning carvers. The Foredom consists of a one-eighth-horsepower motor mounted in a metal housing designed to hang from a shelf or wall bracket. The motor is connected to a hand piece via a flexible shaft, which delivers a no-load speed of 18,000 rpm. The hand piece accepts a wide variety of cutters, ranging from Karbide Kutzall bits that do the work of a hand rasp to small cutters and stones designed for fine work and texturing.

A Foredom kit, consisting of the motor, hand piece, shaft, foot switch, and a variety of cutters, sells for between $200 and $250.

Foredoms hang in more carving shops than any comparable tool being made. Decoy makers use it with a large carbide cutter to rough out bodies and heads, and carvers of decorative birds use it for roughing out as well as for fine work.

The Foredom is not the fastest cutting tool on the market, nor is it the most convenient to use. Because the motor is separate from the hand piece, torque must be supplied via a shaft, which some carvers find cumbersome when doing fine work.

Many professional carvers today use the Foredom for the heavier work, then turn to a faster and more compact tool for detailing. The NSK Electer GX turns at speeds from 1,000 to 40,000 rpm and has the motor

The Foredom is one of the most popular flexible-shaft grinders used by carvers today. The basic bird carving set includes the motor housing, upper right; the hand piece, bottom; and a set of abrasives and cutters.

in the hand piece, thus eliminating the bulky flexible shaft. A light cord connects the hand piece to the control box.

Several manufacturers make high-speed grinders designed for bird carving. Gesswein's Power Carver turns up to 55,000 rpm and offers a variety of hand pieces and accessories. The Paragrave Company of Utah, which specializes in engraving equipment, recently began marketing an air-drive tool for carvers that turns at an incredible 400,000 rpm.

High-speed grinders can make quick work of wood removal, but they are expensive. Expect to pay $700 and up for a basic outfit, plus the cost of the various cutters, burrs, and stones. If you're seriously considering one of these tools, ask a dealer for a demonstration and go with the model that is most comfortable and efficient to use.

Burrs, Cutters, and Stones

Buying a high-speed grinder is like buying a nice stereo system—once all the components are in place, it's time to go out and buy tapes and compact discs and really enjoy your new system. So now that you have your high-speed grinder, it's time to stock up on burrs, cutters, and stones, those invaluable accessories that will enable you to get the most from your new power tool.

High-speed grinders will accept a bewildering variety of accessories. Think of a grinder as an alternative power source. Instead of using the muscles of your hand and wrist, the power is supplied through your local 110-volt outlet. And just as you had to select from a wide variety of hand tools for carving—knives and gouges in an infinite variety of shapes and sizes—so must you select the tools that will be powered by your high-speed grinder.

As with hand tools, selecting the burrs, cutters, and stones to accompany your grinder is a matter of personal choice, dependent upon the type of carving you want to do. The easy way out is to buy a kit. Foredom, for example, offers a ten-piece accessory kit with its #2274 tool designed for wood carvers. Included is a Karbide Kutzall for roughing out, a ruby carver, a vanadium steel carver, and several other cutting and grinding heads. These will get you started, and you can add other designs when the need arises. When buying cutters and stones, select those matched to the speed of your grinder. Using stones at higher speeds than for which they are rated can be dangerous.

The cutting tips used in high-speed grinders vary from the coarse to the refined. Tungsten carbide cutters come in a variety of shapes and remove a great deal of wood in a short time. They approximate the role of the rasp in hand tools, leaving a somewhat rough surface.

Ruby carving bits also come in a variety of shapes and sizes and are used for creating fine detail and for shaping contours. The surface of the bit is made with ruby particles, and it leaves a smooth finish.

Rotary carving burrs made of tungsten vanadium steel are among the most frequently used for bird carving. They also come in a variety of shapes and sizes and are used for many aspects of carving. The larger burrs, called stump cutters, remove wood rapidly but with great control, leaving a smooth surface. Smaller burrs can be used to create contours and to define feather groups.

For precision detailing, diamond carvers are just the thing. You can use them to replicate feathers, ruffles, and folds. They leave an extremely smooth finish and come in a wide variety of shapes.

Abrasive stones are used with a high-speed grinder to create subtle detail. In bird carving your goal is to create the illusion that the surface is not actually made of wood but is soft and pliable, like feathers. This is accomplished not only by carving feather detail—quills, barbs, splits, and so forth—but by creating subtle contours, little tufts that give the illusion of softness. Diamond carvers and stones are used to create layers of feathers, to provide the illusion of loft, to define groupings of feathers. (See the Bird Carving Basics books *Texturing* and *Heads* for specific instructions.) Once these areas are carved, the feather detail is added with a burning tool.

The Burning Tool

Pyrographic pens have been around for a long time. In shop class in high school we made nameplates by burning our signatures into pine planks, which were then stained and varnished.

The pyrographic arts have come a long way since those days. Modern wood-burning systems produce extremely fine lines, making them perfect for carving feather detail.

The burning tool used by bird carvers consists of a sharp blade whose edge is heated to enable it to leave a fine, clean line in wood. While the blade cuts, the heat cauterizes and compresses the wood fibers, producing a well-defined, shallow groove. The finest blades can scribe eighty to one hundred lines per inch.

The better burning tools have a potentiometer to regulate the amount of heat plus interchangeable hand pieces that offer a wide variety of blade profiles. Starter sets provide about 35 watts of power, while the more advanced units hit 100 watts or more and can deliver 2,000 degrees of heat to the tip in less than ten seconds.

Before investing in a burning tool, try various models at carving-supply stores or at carving shows, then pick the one that is most comfortable to use. Expect to pay between $100 and $200 for a good wood-burning system.

Other Tools

As the popularity of bird carving has grown during the last decade, so has the variety of tools available to the carver. High-speed grinders have simplified the business of shaping wood, and burning tools enable the carver to create lifelike feather detail. Frequently, tools used in other disciplines have been adapted to bird carving.

The disk grinder seen frequently in auto body shops is used by carvers to rough out large carvings. A carbide steel wheel on a four-inch grinder will remove a lot of wood quickly. So will the Lancelot cutter, which basically is a chain-saw blade fitted to a four-inch grinder.

The Auto Mach power chisel features a power source connected to a reciprocating hand piece. It does all the work of chisels and gouges but without mallets or muscle power. If you like to work with chisels and gouges but have problems with the physical demands of the tools, a power chisel could be a good investment. Many carvers use the power chisel to rough out a carving. It produces no dust, creates little noise, and removes wood quickly.

No matter how smoothly your new high-speed grinder cuts, you'll still have to do some sanding, and tool manufacturers have come up with a variety of options. Sanding drums are used by many carvers—they make quick work of a hunting-decoy body, removing marks left by the spokeshave or chisel.

Drums can be mounted on a drill or directly on a motor arbor. The drum is made of rubber and can be inflated to provide either a soft or hard surface. Sandpaper is easily replaced by deflating the drum and sliding on a new sanding sleeve.

For small jobs sanding disks can be used with Foredoms and other high-speed grinders. Split mandrels can be used with a small piece of sandpaper to clean up feather contours. A "defuzzer," which looks like a kitchen pot scrubber, can be used on a grinder to smooth and clean the surface of the wood prior to burning feather detail.

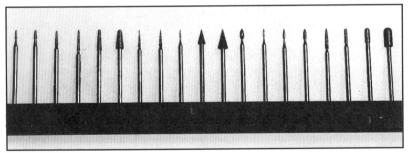

Diamond carvers come in a wide variety of shapes and sizes and are used on high-speed grinders to add fine detail such as feather layers and folds. The hard cutting surface leaves wood smooth.

Ruby carvers are larger than diamond cutters and are designed for heavier work, such as general shaping and creating contours. The ruby-coated surface resists heat buildup and clogging and leaves a smooth surface.

Realistic carving is dependent upon attention to detail. Carvers often work from patterns, taxidermy mounts, or even live birds. It helps to be able to take accurate measurements, and that's where tools such as dial calipers, contour gauges, and dividers come in.

Very often a tool or accessory will be found in an unlikely place. Veteran carvers have a habit of browsing through hardware stores, office-supply stores, art-supply shops, and the housewares section of department stores. Epoxy used in plumbing applications makes a great bird foot. A copper pot scrubber, when torn apart and painted dull green, bears an uncanny resemblance to Spanish moss.

Carving tools are in a process of evolution, as is the field of carving itself. With new artistic ideas come innovations in tools. With new problems come new solutions. The last decade has seen many such solutions. It will be exciting to see what the next ten years bring.

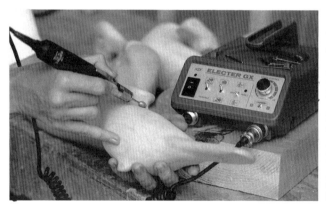

The NSK Electer GX is one of the modern high-speed grinders that include a compact motor in the hand piece, thus eliminating the need for a heavy connecting shaft. The adjustable power control permits speeds from 1,000 to 40,000 rpm. The hand piece accepts shafts of 3/32 inch and 1/8 inch.

The Paragrave Corporation recently introduced its Parapak, a high-speed, air driven carving and engraving instrument designed to work on wood, glass, metal, stone, and other materials. The Parapak system sells for $1,000 to $3,000, depending upon accessories and services purchased with the instrument.

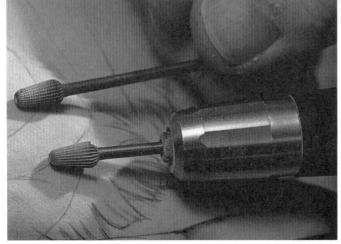

Stump cutters are designed for fast removal of wood but provide a clean cut that is easily controlled. The burr mounted in the hand piece is a fluted stump cutter, and the top burr is a crosshatched version of similar shape. The crosshatched cutter removes wood slower than the stump cutter but leaves a smoother surface.

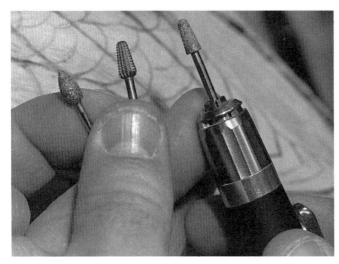

Tips such as these are used by many carvers to create feather groups. The cutter on the left is a ruby carver and is used for rounding off feather edges. The stump cutter, center, is used for general shaping, and the diamond cutter, right, is used to carve fine detail.

The pear-shaped, fluted cutter is used to carve large feather groups, such as those sketched on this carving. The cutter creates subtle valleys between feather groups, giving the impression of softness and loft. Smaller cutters are later used to add fine detail.

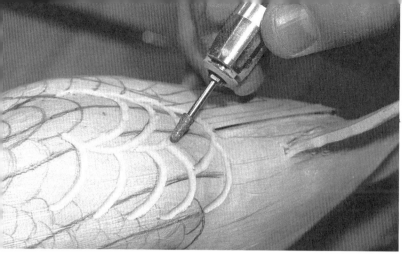

This stone has a slightly rounded tip and is used to define individual feathers on the back and sides of this carving.

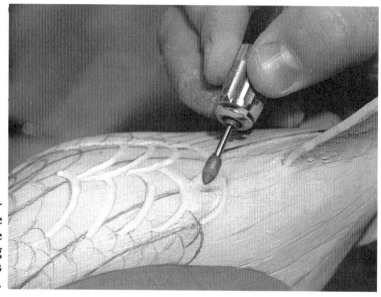

The feathers detailed with the smaller stone are softened along their edges with this larger ruby carver.

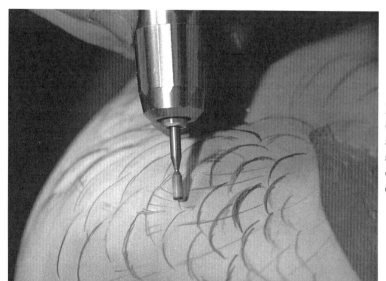

Individual feather detail such as splits are carved with a small, flat-edged cutter such as this diamond carver.

The ruby carver is good for general shaping, such as carving a bill. Rounded stones such as this remove wood fast but do not provide fine detail. Sharp-edged stones are used to etch fine lines. As with chisels and gouges, carvers need cutting tips in a variety of shapes and sizes.

An advantage of the high-speed grinder is that it can remove wood quickly in areas that would be difficult to reach with hand tools. A diamond cutter quickly removes wood from the opened bill in this carving.

This tiny diamond tip is perfect for carving nostrils. The hard edge of the cutting tip and high rpm of the grinder provide a controlled, precise cut.

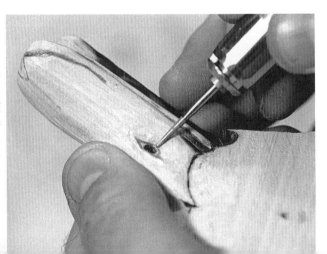

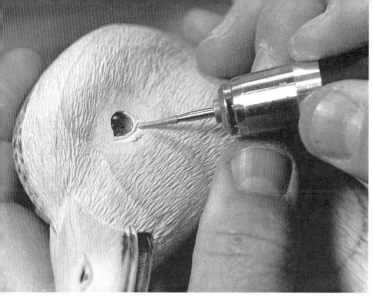

The diamond tip can even carve detail as fine as the eye membrane. The eye was mounted in Plastic Wood and the cutter is actually carving the filler.

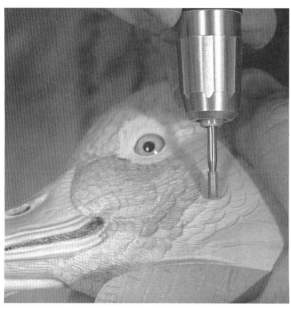

Individual feather barbs can be carved with a flat-edged stone. This diamond cutter leaves a smooth edge.

Once feathers and feather groups are carved, the burning tool is used to add barbs and quills. The burning tool consists of a sharp edge that is heated via a rheostat. The hot tip cauterizes the wood, leaving an extremely smooth cut.

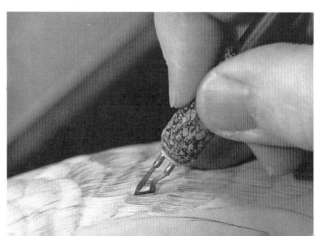

Fine burning tips can carve as many as eighty to one hundred lines per inch. The cork handle insulates the heated element, making the instrument comfortable to use.

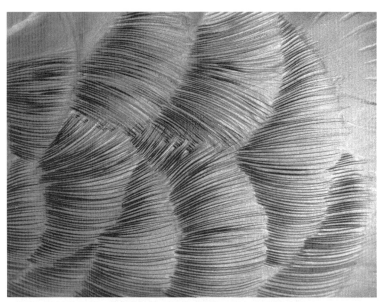

This close-up shows the combined effect of stones and burning tools. The stones were used in a grinder to create feather groups, providing a layered effect, then the burning tool was used to carve each barb and quill. (See Bird Carving Basics, *Texturing*, for details on these procedures.)

The burning tool is not just for carving feather barbs. Here the carver uses it to add detail to an opened bill.

Need to remove wood fast? This four-inch chain-saw disk mounted on a grinder will do the job.

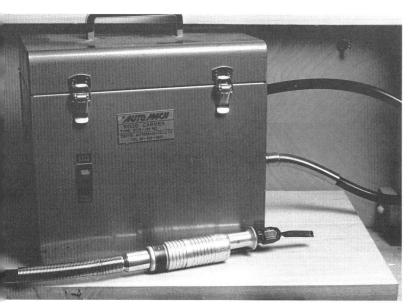

For carvers who like to use chisels and gouges but who don't have the strength and dexterity to properly control the tools, the Auto Mach power chisel can supply the muscle power via electronics.

The power chisel features a rapidly reciprocating blade to provide cutting action with little force necessary on the part of the operator. The tool is quiet and creates no dust.

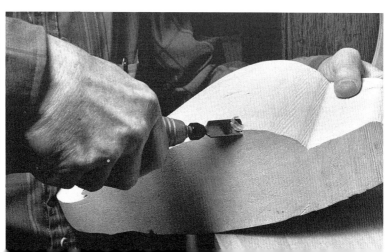

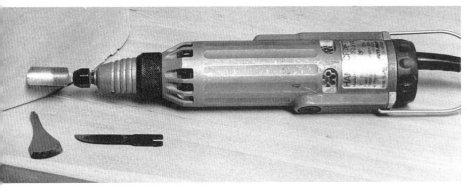

The Auto Mach comes with chisel, gouge, and knife attachments in a variety of shapes.

Sanding is usually necessary at some point in the carving process. An inflatable drum is handy for sanding large pieces. The sanding belt surrounds an inflated rubber sleeve, and you can deflate the sleeve to easily change belts.

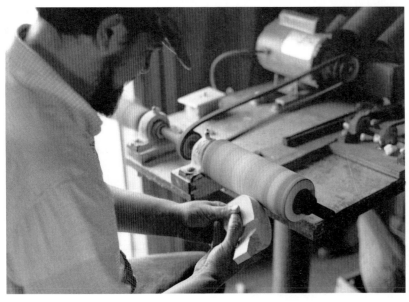

Grayson Chesser rounds out a decoy head on his sanding drum. Care should be taken to avoid breathing dust particles when sanding. Grayson uses an exhaust fan mounted below and to the left of his sander, which pulls dust particles outside the shop.

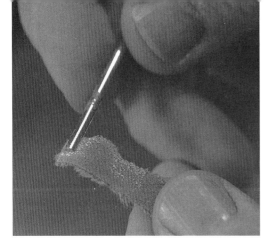

On small carvings sanding can be tedious. A split mandrel mounted on a high-speed grinder will usually do the job.

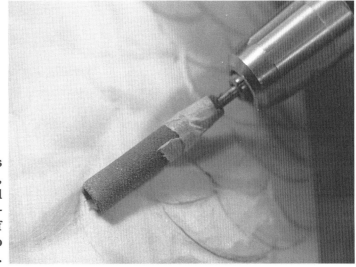

A small piece of sandpaper is threaded through the mandrel, then is taped to form a small cylinder. Sandpaper in a mandrel can be used to round off sharp feather edges and to otherwise subdue detail.

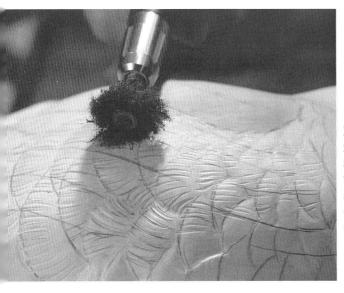

It looks like a pot scrubber from the kitchen, but it's called a defuzzer. It is used to remove wood fibers and to clean and slightly burnish the surface of a carving before adding feather detail with a burning tool.

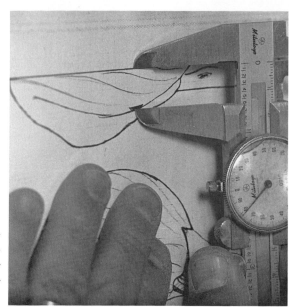

In highly realistic carving, accurate measurements are imperative. Dial calipers help transfer measurements from patterns or study birds to the workpiece.

Calipers are used here to measure the eye channel, checking the dimensions against those of the pattern.

These eye bits, designed to drill holes for the insertion of glass eyes, are specialized drill bits made just for the carver. They come in sizes that correspond with the diameter of glass eyes and include a pilot point for accurate placement.

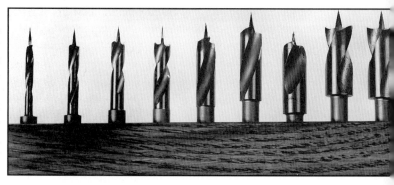

Appendix

Here is a list of sources for tools and carving supplies. It is not a complete list; hundreds of retailers around the country sell tools and other materials that can be used in bird carving. This is something of a starter list, and you will add to it as you gain experience.

A good up-to-date source for carving tools and supplies is the advertising section in *Wildfowl Carving and Collecting* magazine, published by Stackpole Books (P.O. Box 1831, Harrisburg, PA 17105). In the pages of the magazine you can compare prices and specifications without leaving your easy chair or workbench.

Another good source is the network of carvers that exists around the country and, indeed, throughout the world. Join a carving club, attend a seminar, go to a competition or exhibition. You'll meet dozens of people who share the same interests and goals, and you'll learn where to find that special stone or knife or how to solve a perplexing carving problem.

Sources: Tools and Supplies

Jack Andrews, 1482 Maple Ave., Paoli, PA 19301. Wood-carving knives and knife kits.

Colwood Electronics, 1 Meridian Rd., Eatontown, NJ 07724. Wood-burning tools.

Craftwoods, 2101-B Greenspring Dr., Timonium, MD 21093. 800-468-7070. Wide variety of carving tools and supplies.

Curt's Waterfowl Corner, P.O. Box 228, Montegut, LA 70377. 800-523-8474. Wide variety of tools and supplies.

The Duck Blind, 8721 Gull Rd., Richland, MI 49083. 800-852-7352. Wide variety of carving supplies.

P. C. English, Inc., P.O. Box 380, Thornburg, VA 22565. 800-221-9474. Wide variety of carving supplies.

Foredom Electric Co., Bethel, CT 06801. Foredom flexible-shaft grinders.

Forest Products, P.O. Box 12, Avon, OH 44011. Basswood carving kits, various supplies and tools.

Gesswein, 255 Hancock Ave., Bridgeport, CT 06605. 800-544-2043, ext. 22. High-speed grinders.

Godin Art, P.O. Box 62, Brantford, Ontario, Canada N3T 5M3. Patterns, instructional videos, painting supplies by artist Pat Godin.

Jennings Decoy Co., 601 Franklin Ave. NE, St. Cloud, MN 56304. 800-331-5613. Carving kits, general tools and supplies.

Little Mountain Supply, Inc., Rt. 2, Box 1329, Bowling Green Rd., Front Royal, VA 22630. Wide variety of carving tools and supplies.

Navesink Electronics, 381 Nut Swamp Rd., Red Bank, NJ 07701. Wood-burning system.

Paragrave Corp., 1455 W. Center St., Orem, UT 84057. 800-624-7415. Parapak air-drive cutting tool.

Manuel Ramos, Sr., Virginia Grinding and Equipment Co., 3205B Tait Terrace, Norfolk, VA 23513. Specialists in sharpening knives, drawknives, and gouges.

Schoepfer Eyes, 138 West 31st St., New York, NY 10001. Glass eyes.

J. D. Sprankle, 221 Gunners Rest Lane, Chester, MD 21619. Study birds, painting supplies, carving seminars, videos.

Warren Tool Co., 2209-1 Route 9G, Rhinebeck, NY 12572. Carving knives.

Waterfowl Study Bills, P.O. Box 310, Evergreen, LA 71333. Cast study bills.

Woodcraft, 210 Wood County Industrial Park, P.O. Box 1686, Parkersburg, WV 26102. 800-225-1153. Wide variety of carving and woodworking supplies.

About the Author

Curtis Badger has written widely about wild-fowl art, wildfowl hunting, and conservation issues in general. His articles have appeared in many national and regional magazines, and he has served as editor of *Wildfowl Art Journal*. He is the co-author of *Painting Waterfowl with J. D. Sprankle*, which is also available from Stackpole. He lives near the town of Onancock, Virginia.

Other Books of Interest to Bird Carvers

How to Carve Wildfowl
The masterful techniques of nine international blue-ribbon winners.
by Roger Schroeder

How to Carve Wildfowl Book 2
Features eight more master carvers and the tools, paints, woods, and techniques they use for their best-in-show carvings.
by Roger Schroeder

Waterfowl Carving with J. D. Sprankle
A fully illustrated reference to carving and painting 25 decorative ducks.
by Roger Schroeder and James D. Sprankle

Painting Waterfowl with J. D. Sprankle
Over 400 spectacular color photos illustrate this incomparable painting guide. Includes step-by-step instruction for 13 projects and color charts for exact paint mixes.
by Curtis J. Badger and James D. Sprankle

Making Decoys the Century-Old Way
Detailed, step-by-step instructions on hand-making the simple yet functional working decoys of yesteryear.
by Grayson Chesser and Curtis J. Badger

Decorative Decoy Designs
Bruce Burk's three volumes (*Dabbling and Whistling Ducks*, *Diving Ducks*, and *Geese and Swans*) are complete guides to decoy painting by a renowned master of the art. All three feature life-size color patterns, reference photographs, alternate position patterns, and detailed paint-mixing instructions.
by Bruce Burk

John Scheeler, Bird Carver
A tribute to the bird-carving world's master of master, John Scheeler.
by Roger Schroeder

Carving Miniature Wildfowl with Robert Guge
Scale drawings, step-by-step photographs and painting keys demonstrate the techniques that make Guge's miniatures the best in the world.
by Roger Schroeder and Robert Guge

Songbird Carving with Ernest Muehlmatt
Muehlmatt shares his expertise on painting, washes, feather flicking, and burning, plus insights on composition, design, proportion, and balance.
by Roger Schroeder and Ernest Muehlmatt

For complete ordering information, write:
Stackpole Books
P.O. Box 1831
Harrisburg, PA 17105
or call 1-800-732-3669